YOU ARE A UNICORN

THE FUN CREATIVE JOURNAL FOR EVERYONE!

BLACK
dot books

instagram.com/YouAreAUnicornBook

First published 2017 by Black Dot Books,
an imprint of Souper Media Limited.

This collection © Souper Media Limited 2017

ISBN 978-1544118987
ISBN 1544118988

Printed by CreateSpace

HELLO THERE!

Thanks for being interested enough in my book to take the time to read this. The chances are you're looking at *You Are A Unicorn* because you're interested in becoming more creative and want to zap some positivity into your life. Well, good news – you've come to the right place!

The awesome activities in this book will help unlock your imagination, release your creativity and boost the way you feel – they're fun and relaxing too!

The pages of *You Are A Unicorn* may just be paper, but with your input they'll soon be brimming with amazing ideas and brilliant stuff only YOU can create. So this book's really a collaboration – I've done my bit, and now it's up to you to do yours.

So get set to release your inner unicorn, and scribble, list, create, share and clip-clop your way to happiness – *You Are A Unicorn* after all.

Good luck on your adventures – let's get going!

VINCENT VINCENT

DRAW A SELF PORTRAIT

FiLL THiS PAGE WiTH SCRiBBLES

LiKE THiS!

TOP 10 TREATS

1)

2)

3)

4)

5)

6)

7)

8)

9)

10)

I AM BRILLIANT BECAUSE...

* TELL THE WORLD WHY
   YOU'RE AMAZING!

FILL THESE BALLOONS WITH FEELINGS

MY BEST FRIEND IS...

*DESCRIBE
YOUR BFF!

MY FAVOURITE WORDS ARE....

THE BEST BOOKS I'VE
EVER READ ARE...

FILL THIS PAGE WITH THINGS THE WORLD NEEDS MORE OF!

DRAW AN AWESOME UNICORN

I want to...

** *
DRAW YOUR
LUCKY CHARM!

WRITE A LIST OF PEOPLE WHO MAKE YOU HAPPY!

MY FAMILY THINK I AM...

WORDS THAT MAKE
ME LAUGH ARE...

DRAW A PICTURE OF AN ANIMAL YOU LOVE

TOP 10 COLOURS

1)

2)

3)

4)

5)

6)

7)

8)

9)

10)

THE FIRST THING YOU THOUGHT
ABOUT TODAY WAS...

I DON'T CARE ABOUT...

FILL THIS PAGE WITH
DOODLES OF CLOUDS

I AM GOING TO BE...

THESE THINGS
ARE IN MY BAG...

*DRAW WHATEVER
IS IN YOUR BAG!

MY GOALS FOR THE DAY ARE...

FiLL THiS PAGE WiTH THiS POSITiVE SENTENCE...

I am creative

Encouraging words can help boost our confidence, enthusiasm and general well-being. Next time someone pays you a compliment, thank them and write down what they say on this page. Never forget – you're amazing!

PEOPLE TELL ME I'M *GOOD* AT...

Fave ice cream flavours

FILL THIS BOX
WITH THINGS YOU
WANT TO CHANGE

LIST YOUR FAVOURITE FEEL GOOD SONGS!

LOL!

HEHE!

HAHA!

HEHE!

DRAW SOMETHING
THAT HAS MADE YOU
LAUGH RECENTLY...

LOL!

POSITIVITY CHECKLIST

- ☐ IDEAS
- ☐ HOPES
- ☐ GOALS
- ☐ HEROES
- ☐ LAUGHTER
- ☐ LESSONS
- ☐ OPTIMISM
- ☐ RELAXATION
- ☐ SUPPORT
- ☐ DREAMS
- ☐ ENERGY

* FILL THIS PAGE WITH DOODLES OF TROPHIES

YOU'RE A WINNER!

MAKE A LIST OF PLACES YOU WANT TO GO

I WANT TO LEARN TO...

TOP 5 FEARS

1)

2)

3)

4)

5)

NOW DRAW THEM HERE

FILL THIS HOLE WITH YOUR PET PEEVES

* THEN SCRIBBLE THEM OUT TO
BANISH THEM FROM YOUR LIFE!

I feel sad when I...

DIVE INTO YOUR IMAGINATION & DRAW WHAT YOU FIND...

* DESCRIBE A
BRILLIANT DAY...

LIST THINGS THAT MAKE YOU

10 WAYS YOU'VE CHANGED IN THE LAST YEAR...

1)

2)

3)

4)

5)

6)

7)

8)

9)

10)

I AM PROUD OF...

TAPE SOMETHING SPECIAL TO THIS PAGE!

DRAW SOMETHING MAGICAL

My goals for
The week are...

HAPPY excited BORED
cool
anxious SAD grumpy
CONTENT WOW SURPRISED
CREATIVE iNSPiRED FRESH
ARTY cheerful GOOD FREE
FUN loved EMOTiONAL
PROMISING awful ENERGISED
GREAT
READY RELAXED GiGGLY
POSITIVE sleepy DREAMY
iNTERESTED
HURT relieved
CURiOUS

CIRCLE THE WORDS THAT SUM UP HOW YOU ARE FEELING TODAY

DESCRIBE THE LAST DREAM
YOU CAN REMEMBER...

MAKE A LIST OF ALL THE REASONS YOU ARE AMAZING

THINGS I'VE...   ...LOST

10 FACTS ABOUT ME

1

2

3

4

5

6

7

8

9

10

LIST THE THINGS
YOU LOVE ABOUT
YOUR FAMILY

* FILL THIS PAGE WITH
DOODLES OF SNOWFLAKES!

DESCRIBE THE VIEW FROM YOUR WINDOW

3

THREE THINGS YOU'D LIKE TO
CHANGE ABOUT YOUR LIFE

10 WAYS YOU CAN HELP YOUR FRIENDS...

1)

2)

3)

4)

5)

6)

7)

8)

9)

10)

WHERE
WOULD YOU LIKE
TO BE IN FIVE
YEARS?

COLOUR
IN THIS
MAGICAL
RAINBOW

THEN WRITE
* OR DRAW
A BIG WISH
AT THE END
OF IT!

- DESCRIBE HOW YOU FEEL WHEN YOU'RE SURROUNDED BY NATURE

THiNGS i AM GRATEFUL FOR...

DESCRIBE A CHALLENGE YOU CONQUERED...

FILL THIS PAGE WITH THIS POSITIVE SENTENCE...

I am happy

LiST 5 ANiMALS YOU LOVE

1)

2)

3)

4)

5)

NOW
DRAW
THEM
HERE!

SMILE!

* FILL THIS PAGE WITH DOODLES OF HAPPY FACES *

I AM
PASSIONATE
ABOUT...

WHAT WOULD YOUR UNICORN POWERS BE?

Do One Day wish list

Got stuff you'd like to do one day? The first step to achieving goals is to recognise them, so make a list of all the fun things you'd like to do. You don't have to do everything right now, but taking this first step is a move in the right direction. Your Do One Day wish list is a record of your future potential!

FRUIT i LiKE

HIGHLIGHT
OF MY YEAR
SO FAR!

List 12 things you like about yourself

1)

2)

3)

4)

5)

6)

7)

8)

9)

10)

11)

12)

I FEEL HAPPY WHEN I...

WRITE DOWN EVERYTHING YOU
DON'T WANT IN YOUR LIFE...

 * THEN CIRCLE IT ALL AND PUT IT IN THE TRASH!

WRITE A LETTER TO YOURSELF TWO YEARS AGO

COVER THIS PAGE
WITH DOODLES OF
CIRCLES!

WHAT'S
ON YOUR
MIND?

MY FAVOURITE
PLACES ARE...

I WISH...

* FILL THIS PAGE
WITH WISHES!

MY FAVOURiTE SOUNDS...

10 HOPES FOR THE FUTURE

1)

2)

3)

4)

5)

6)

7)

8)

9)

10)

WHAT IF...

FILL THIS PAGE WITH THIS POSITIVE SENTENCE...

I am confident

I AM CURRENTLY

☐ READING..................

☐ PLAYING..................

☐ WATCHING..................

☐ STARTING..................

☐ TEXTING..................

☐ LOVING..................

☐ ENJOYING..................

☐ FRIENDS WITH..................

☐ LOL-ING ABOUT..................

☐ EATING..................

☐ DRINKING..................

☐ FINISHING..................

* THE WORLD SEES ME AS...

DRAW A PICTURE OF YOUR DREAM PET

My friends like me because...

LIST 5 THINGS YOU'RE SCARED OF

1

2

3

4

5

FILL THIS PAGE
WITH DOODLES OF
BOXES!

FILL THE TOP HALF OF THIS PAGE WITH THINGS HOLDING YOU BACK...

THEN FILL THE REST OF THE PAGE WITH WAYS TO OVERCOME THEM!

MY GOALS FOR THE MONTH ARE...

10 THINGS YOU LIKE ABOUT BEING OUTDOORS

1)

2)

3)

4)

5)

6)

7)

8)

9)

10)

i CAN ALWAYS
RELY ON...

FILL THIS PAGE WITH THIS POSITIVE SENTENCE...

I am clever

LIST NEGATIVE
STUFF YOU'VE
FELT RECENTLY

* THEN SCRIBBLE OUT THE
WORDS TO ERASE THE NEGATIVITY!

1 2 3 4 5 6 7 8 9 10

* FILL THIS PAGE
WITH DOODLES OF
YOUR FAVOURITE
NUMBER!

PEOPLE YOU ADMIRE...

This page is for the people you admire. Everyone who's ever inspired or encouraged you. Draw them, doodle their names or write a message to them, saying stuff you've never been able to say in person. Other people believe in you and it's great to recognise that!

PERSONAL FILE

FIRST NAME _ _ _ _ _ _ _ _ _ _

AGE _ _ _ _ _ _ _ _ _ _ _

NICKNAME _ _ _ _ _ _ _ _

FAMILY _ _ _ _ _ _ _ _ _

STAR SIGN _ _ _ _ _ _ _ _

HOBBIES _ _ _ _ _ _ _ _ _

PETS _ _ _ _ _ _ _ _ _ _

FRIENDS _ _ _ _ _ _ _ _ _

FUN FACT _ _ _ _ _ _ _ _

SECRET _ _ _ _ _ _ _ _ _

FAVOURITE TV SHOWS

DRAW A PIC OF A TIME YOU FELT LEFT OUT

YOUR BEST FEATURES ARE...

DESCRIBE YOUR BEST FRIEND IN 10 WORDS...

THEN DRAW A PICTURE OF THEM!

COME UP WITH A CRAZY INVENTION AND DRAW IT ON THIS PAGE!

MY FAVOURITE DRINKS ARE...

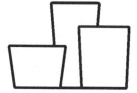

CIRCLE THE WORDS THAT DESCRIBE YOU BEST

ADVENTUROUS FEARLESS
CHEERFUL Gentle
LOVING FAIR
FUNNY CALM CREATIVE
LOUD
alert CLEVER PATIENT
GOOD WARM strong
HONEST BRAVE EXCITED
LIVELY POPULAR
GENEROUS
AMBITIOUS GOOD FUN CARING
RELIABLE
POWERFUL friendly LOYAL
ENTHUSIASTIC DARING Optimistic
HELPFUL KIND BRIGHT POLITE
peaceful OPEN IMAGINATIVE
ENERGETIC trusting SKILLFUL
brilliant DETERMINED happy

YOUR TOP 10 APPS...

1)

2)

3)

4)

5)

6)

7)

8)

9)

10)

LIST 5 THINGS THAT MAKE YOU HAPPY

1

2

3

4

5

*LOVE THIS PAGE!

Your strengths are...

*LIST ALL THE THINGS
YOU'RE GOOD AT!

FiLL THiS PAGE WiTH DOODLES OF YOUR FAVOURITE NAMES...

PEOPLE YOU LOVE AND WHY...

WHERE WOULD YOU LIKE TO BE IN 10 YEARS?

YOUR TOP 10 FAVOURITE SNACKS ARE...

1)

2)

3)

4)

5)

6)

7)

8)

9)

10)

FILL THESE JARS WITH WORDS THAT MEAN SOMETHING SPECIAL TO YOU...

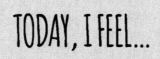

TODAY, I FEEL...

HAPPINESS CHECKLIST

☐   ☐

☐   ☐

☐   ☐

☐   ☐

☐   ☐

☐   ☐

☐   ☐

☐   ☐

☐   ☐

☐   ☐

* Make a list of everything that makes you happy. Then tick off each thing from the list that you already have in your life. This will help remind you of all of the fantastic stuff you have – and what to be thankful for!

MY
EARLIEST
MEMORIES
ARE...

WRITE DOWN 10
THINGS YOU NEED

YOUR DREAM
JOBS ARE...

THINGS I ENJOY DOING FOR OTHER PEOPLE....

1)

2)

3)

4)

5)

6)

7)

8)

9)

10

10)

THiNGS YOU'RE
AWESOME AT...

FILL THIS PAGE WITH DOODLES OF STARS!

FILL THIS PAGE WITH THIS POSITIVE SENTENCE...

I am special

WHAT SUPER POWERS WOULD YOU LIKE?

WHAT STUFF HAS GONE WRONG RECENTLY?

MY GOALS FOR
THE YEAR ARE...

WRITE A SHORT STORY ABOUT A FRIEND

WHAT STUFF HAS GONE RiGHT RECENTLY?

10
THINGS NO
ONE KNOWS
ABOUT ME

FILL THIS BOX
WITH COOL STUFF
IN YOUR LIFE

LIST 15 THINGS THAT EXCITE YOU!

FILL THIS PAGE WITH
DOODLES OF CATS AND DOGS!

I WISH THE WORLD
DIDN'T HAVE...

FILL THIS PAGE WITH THINGS THAT MAKE YOU HAPPY

LIST YOUR FAVOURITE FEEL GOOD FILMS!

10 THINGS YOU WANT

1)

2)

3)

4)

5)

6)

7)

8)

9)

10)

DOODLE THE FIRST THING THAT COMES INTO YOUR HEAD

NO1

DESCRIBE YOUR NUMBER ONE PLACE IN THE WORLD

DESCRIBE YOUR LIFE IN 10 WORDS

1

2

3

4

5

6

7

8

9

10

FILL IN THE SPEECH BUBBLES WITH STUFF YOU'D LIKE TO SAY TO SOMEONE BUT CAN'T

TODAY I FEEL...

*INVENT NEW
WORDS
FOR THINGS AND
FILL THIS PAGE
WITH THEM

DESCRIBE YOUR MOST EMBARRASSING MOMENT!

HOW i MET MY BEST FRIEND....

FILL THIS PAGE WITH THIS POSITIVE SENTENCE...

I am awesome

LIST THE PEOPLE WHO MAKE YOU LOL!

DESCRIBE THE WORLD TO AN ALIEN!

THEN DESCRIBE YOUR LIFE!

FILL THIS PAGE
WITH DOODLES OF
SOMETHING YOU
LOVE!

SHARE YOUR FEELINGS
ON THIS PAGE

YOUR 5 BEST MOMENTS SO FAR

1)

2)

3)

4)

5)

NOW PLAN THE NEXT 5!

GET DOODLING AND FILL
THIS PAGE WITH HEARTS!

5 WAYS YOU'VE CHANGED SINCE YOU STARTED THIS BOOK...

LOOK OUT
FOR MORE BOOKS
IN THIS RANGE
SOON!

BLACK
dot books

73219312R00093

Made in the USA
Middletown, DE
12 May 2018